Bric-a-Brack

Gemma Tambling

Bric-a-Brack,
not so dissimilar to the former
Bric-a-Brac.
My own version brought about
after my time spent
in Brackendale psych ward in 2015.
Tribulations like these
have laid the foundations
of this book.
My spine has long carried the belief
that I am housed by fragments
of little to no value,
the sum of my parts inessential,
like a table dressing up the bric-a-brac
in last attempts
before waste-claimed.
I am still scribing poetry
that desires to be more than a bruise,
a landmark of my experiences
exalted to the grandeur of healing.
I pray this journey that you take with me
will relight purpose,
so that you may meet comfortably
in the process
of your crawl spaces gracing light,
a refraction birthed by newfound faith.

You, the reader,
seeking escape—
step into these pages:
bare-foot and unguarded.
Remove by its fraying ends,
the noose you have let asphyxiate your being
to a submission, too long.
My noose was tied by a list of names.
Each chapter I unbind piece by piece
—the past, the future—
what I cannot control.
Find comfort in every descent
your fingers take travelling through these pages;
you are coming home to yourself, home to your hope.

Some of the most profoundly moving individuals I know,
believed they were nothing more than collective bodies,
taking up too much space.

For the scars that littered only to heal,
and the healing that has yet to begin

Pitstop Men

There it began, the tender age, alerted to hands
yielding touch far too long.

Your fingers bite into me
as teeth tear the flesh of a peach,
you demand I be sweeter
but this blood calls of fear,
devoured by iron
disgusted I leak like tears.

All I ask
is an uncle, a cousin
to patch the holes punched
into me, an infant
grown to the touch
of poison hands
and how they sear still
in their absence.

A male to touch my heart
and not beneath my clothes.

Some nights drunk
from lack of sleep
searching for your shadow,
the particular fit that warns
of impending danger.

The kind I search for now,
even in a home so silent
I could map the travels
of rain down windows.

The only lollipop I knew of
was not that of a gift
at a dentist's office,
my infant self
torn in the places
families were supposed to heal.

Sit pretty,
but not like that.

Your demands
a crescendo
under the crushing weight,
your illusions of perfection.

Rising and falling,
in strides, I tried
to meet delusion in the middle.

The willing branches of your arms
placing me in a manner, proper,
propagating the belief
I am only as beautiful
as how my back, arched
profits a gaze from a stranger
three times my senior,
his eyes burrowed cold
into the crooks of my skin,
as though I am a cheque
yet to be cashed.

His love was that of a forcefield,
consuming visuals of others
with idle attempt to conceal.

Nightly, hands housing rage,
making contact
as a fist would to drywall,
his words in vehement
pulling the life out of me,
in tufts that slowly
unraveled my spine through my back.

His slurs of love
becoming all too obscured
by his tempestuous mouth,
words spat in familiar fury.

Similar apologies
rolling off his snakeskin tongue,
laced as thick as his daily venom,
my soul found rebirth
bathed by sweetest delight,
I reclaimed my pieces
and we packed that night.

To insist a woman's body
must fit a mould
to be deemed worthy,
of all you in strides
would only fail to give her.

No matter how open
your disregard for her is,
in order to lure her
by picking insecurities
like apple's from a tree,
you'll never satiate her.

She is an ocean floor
who holds and calms
she may settle the shores,
but she would never settle for you.

When the air calls
and you feel bruised
beneath cotton layers
may you never trust
that foul things
are to be fair.

I washed my hair,
the water dripping
off my skin
removing
traces of you,
yet
your fingertips
remained on me
from within.

You,
are my number thirteen.

The reason to hold all reasons
absolute.

Trembling are my foundations
once strong.

You touched
with a forbidden hand,
a pain that dived deep
inside of me,
ejecting a soul
from a crying body.

I was limber
under your scorched hands.

The kind of fragile that declared
the innocence of my youth.

Rocking an Angel in your grasp,
I hope your stomach grows thorns
and you are pricked of the knowledge
that you are a stealer
number thirteen,

your theft knows no bounds.

*JAIL SIN
AND
SEX HANDS.*

You have a mouth
like poison
a tongue like prison,
hands that
bend and weave
through my
fragile spines.

Temporary Home
I was housed
between
the burning bridges
of your hands.

Ghosts Don't Bode Well To Showers
I'd long forgotten
your skin impressions,
yet I wore them every night.

Stunted Growth
He played with me
like growing up
was not an option.

Saving for a mortgage
a man to finally
bid my body right,

you took my values
monetary and otherwise
investing
in your holiday home,
tempered and fleeting.

You curved your finger into me
even then I met the inquisition.

Tell the man
with the hook he has manned,
that he still carries my heart
in the palm of his gunmetal hand

If you see him, let him know
I've paid quite the toll
and I shall wait at his port,
though he bares not a thought

his white sails my night-light,
because half of a whole
is enough still to fight.

The slow hum
of the lampshade
crooked and cradling
the floor,
my fingers musing
in memory
of the night before.

The moon has heard
the wails, the shrieks,
the unsteady whimpers,
the pin drop silence
in anticipation of footsteps
that were not my own,
but all too familiar
as though they could be.

Salacious,
the nightly wolf
preened, a coat
of many a crimson
victory,
its boastful pride
lays tongue silent
to the pack
leading his lone,
daylight cowardice astray.

Our veins shed similar blood
but you held not a breath
of discomfort
to see me bleeding,
broken under you.

Can you hear my footsteps
blading through your sanctuary?
Pulsing restitution.

Grapple it I shall,
'til your spine breaks splinters,
'til your lungs know not of air,
'til your tongue does not romanticize
the flesh of kin.

You have a darker taste for midnight stealing,
but I wear moonlight like a phoenix sun
emblazoned by all you tried thieve,
karma beats light from my lion mouth,
honey drips a forgiveness,
knowing your pallid heart
and prison hands
leave you more emptied
than I.

I lay silent,
clutching the sheets
hoping my flickering eyes,
tightly closed
wouldn't stir in you a fever,
recognition I was sprung awake
by your footsteps on the stairs
closing distance to my room.
When you took my photograph
you stole my childhood soul,
not only had you claimed my flesh
you sewed it to permanence,
hands missing my thighs,
brushing my underwear aside
to capture your depravity.
I remember it still,
how you shook.
I cannot make peace
that you shared more with excitement
than my fear.

My words form the jurors,
body, the condemning trial
the term I face, a life-sentence
my fear serves as delight upon you,
these silences bed you in safety,
but I now cannot contort my body
for lovers,
without feeling the spiked ridges
of your hands, shaking,
driven by the fleshy trauma
you sewed into me
as kin.

These words break my silence,
I unravel them,
along with guilt,
shame, discontent.

I have far too long discarded events,
hushed them to comfort
the heartbreak of loved ones,
I may not be public in my pursuits
to bring you to your knees
as you had me do,
karma does not wilt
at the hands of the law,
and I will no longer
serve your punishment.

— *She will*

My Mother's Earth

Mother Earth

Softly
as rain travels
down the spines of leaves,
I pine under palm trees
cradling the essence of earth,
oh, how a mother
could both
create and collide.

35

Her hands
were a pillow of cells
keeping out disquiet.

And that was the moment
I knew I would pack up and run,
but I would not be alone
for she ran better than I.

It was not okay,
but my mother
made it so.

The Things My Mother Said
We have not wealth but love,
be it all we need.

She Oughta Know
You pulled me
out of myself,
and back
into home.

The Truth That Hurt
You'll get over it,
her words bruised.

My Mother served no platitudes,
she spoke of healing
like a career
that paid off slowly,
rewards reaped
only years after
the benefits
of thought numbing labour
had long outgrown
the suffering.

When the Earth lays
thick blankets of snow,
I think of my mama.

How her hair of grey hues
always catches the morning,
as though it is patting gently away
her bedraggled strands,
a symptom of disquieting sleep.

Silently she ponders
how her love has amassed
four children,
who, to her heart's woe
would struggle maintaining face
in her absence.

The truth is,
I know that her snow
will not blanket long,
and the sun would shine still,
in her absence,
but I find no solace
in the earth's continuity to thrive
amidst my internal wars,
mother earth
could not calm me
like her.

It is not your fault
that hands have crept inside me,
planting thorns between each visit,
I know you know not
how to pick them out,
you do not know how to understand
how an innocent cried to you
a blurb of her assault,
at the eve of her sixth birthday.

You prefer my pages
in a language you can't read.

I know your bated breath
did not believe
my story was as cruel
as my fingers traced it,
childhood skin the canvas,

and it was not because
you believed me a liar,
I know
your heart cracked
in your chest
because you knew
the wolf only had to knock
to come in.

You do not like flowers
but if I could show you
how soft your arms feel
around my brokenness,
I would form chains of daisies
at your feet
for when walking beside me
draws blisters.

Your summer bloom
a full-thresh glory
meeting the eyes of autumn
with a billowing head
and coy lips,
cosying
to the preparing
winter
as she lays
her first cast.

She reminds me
that we too
have our seasonal shades,
the colours most seek from us,
but only few receive.

You carried me.

Even when your path
no longer entwines with mine
still, you'll carry me.

What I Know of Love

The bees tell me
the highlights in your hair
fall like honey.

My eyes roll in response,

water white

or

amber?

If you won't touch my heart
the same way you caress my hair,
why do you touch me
like you'll stay?

I wish you could give my body
the love it craves
not the lust that has taken
it without permission,
I'm passed the eve
but not yet prime,
clock bites into my ears
with each second
I am touched of the knowledge
love was not enough
to keep you from trafficking
the demands of crying women
as day broke,
and hearing them again
as night roared in your ears
to stop the scraping of your fingers.

I lay awake
painting
versions of us
on the ceiling,
a tapestry
nightly falling
to blanket me
in its blushed satin,
my skin finds home
underneath illustrations,
perhaps these delusions
speak more of my heart
than my mind.

She's the oil lamp
lit with the purpose
of burning
the reaches
of my darkness,
though it is I
who craves more
when the embers dim out.

Why must we learn bodies
before we learn minds—
before we learn purpose?

As though the flick of a finger
could satiate the need for love,
as though lust, much like a spear
to the groin,
could leave us
as filled as truth should.

She was the echo
of a fire,

the roaring
of winter's wind,

the content
breath of lovers,

as they lay
their armour down

in place of love
which graces endless.

Her hair
bouncing shapely
as bare feet
navigate
through the weed-like
flux
of the garden

I knew
even then,
as she waltzed in front
to music
I couldn't hear,
that where she stood,
sat, breathed,
would be home to me.

I liked the dark.
Namely, how our love settled
underneath the covers.
We lay awake,
nestled into each other,
as though breathing
would be deemed impossible
if it were not so.
The hemisphere we were lucky
to share — deftly unaware
of a passion burning the sheets
on a coarse night in October.

I could almost hear the moon
peeling back the furnishings
of adjoined roofs
to witness
the miracle its night could clad,
amongst lovers perfectly unclad.

I'll go down
as if your body
is the reason
I'm breathing.

Some days I hate you
until I remember
this hole you left
was so you could
mend your own.

I almost forgot how
your empty
shampoo bottles
decorated the place
better
than I've ever done,
every attempt
after you
merely littered.

Our lips taste similarly
the burdens that estrange us,
leaving us captors to murky pillows
that which we are not used to,
exposing the fragilities
we house.

We reek of smiles long faded,
arms too numb and jaded,
pill-popping phenomenon
yet not a soul understands,
but you, fine beauty
catch glimpse of my relapsing
and offer up your hand.

I'm lonely,
and I miss her.
Not the her
usual to my longing.
The girl with the long locks
soft as satin, to shaved legs.
A brazen beauty
I refused to let get close,
but it's almost 2am
and her fiery hair
dancing like a candle
at a concert
she knows little words to,
has enveloped me.

Now my world is of autumnal hues
eyes a looking glass,
admiring her golden gaze
from my peripherals.

Sunday's
of bittersweet
disservice.

Timelines
could not be
more watchful
than the shifting
of my eyes to clock.

Palms fumbling hair,
messily
I'm left detangling
the knots.

You bid a goodbye,
one of many
this damned Sunday.

The approach of weekend
leaving weekday in array,
as now I belong to you
until this turning Sunday.

Palm to comb,
dragging out moments,
reverie blushing my skin,
your hands coupled
in our longing.

Tales of sorrow
bed our hair.

In awe of this,
still, I cannot resist
as we claim boldly,
our Sunday's
and grow weak
from last kiss.

The eve of this day
more impassioned than any,
still I render it
incompletely
from the hums
of our ecstasy.

Those hard to swallow
lyrics
are not so
from their emptying
truths,
but
the lulls in reading,
where I notice
a family stayed
given the divide
of my mind's tangent
to die —
yet I crave notice
from the stranger
of twelve months
who left void words
at the eve of my neck,
how I chose to believe
the synchronicity of lightness
beating out your throat,
as though it were usual
to speak of love
like a monotonous drum.

I had to bare thought
summer would not long be here
and you had not
packed for the winter.

I still wear the perfume
you bought
under my naked skin
tell me,
does it touch you
in the places
it touches me?

You gave them a moment in time,
you gave me moments perpetual.

My first love taught me
how to swallow pills
in the eve of his wandering hands
and the dawn of his aggression.

He taught me not all people
carry morals as they would their passports,
tightly bound and open to explore.

The only exploring I knew
was of his side-eye adventures
that beckoned my body
to a halt.

But of all things taught
I had been holding farce,
he would forever pale
in my future pursuits—
for in my venture for love,
a woman
poured to me
her heart.

— the moment I realised my roots.

The honey on your mouth
roused my taut lips
to drink,

you offered up
your fountain tongue

in exchange,
I'd only ever drink there.

My thighs brush your cheek,
the delight you savour
running down your chin
in our maple syrup mornings.

Needs straddled,
hands in fists,
fingernails bound so tightly
into palms,
I clench in contortion.

The only honey
sweet enough
to hold a craving
long after it's dealt.

Tectonic plates moving,
full throttle in my unrest
did I delve the corpse
of your shifting city.

Touching your worn spaces
long grazed by the storm
before I.

Settled midpoint the Earth
where the sun shone brighter
on your battlefield flesh,
navigating my hands
blading like grass
to hold you
in the aftermath.

Blistered feet sigh my defeat
giving up coupled to greet me
in hymns of low lulls,

met with ocean waves
inside my brain
the cold crept in again,

the kindness of a stranger
passing by with kin
lent me a glimpse of hope again.

W.B.Yeats paperback
pages rolling in place of regret,
off of my numb, cold hands
traipsing the edges as though
it was freeing to be cut.

I hope the eve of your morning
can stretch around me,
a lily coloured sunlight
illuminating my hair
from the window,
the only specks I allow
to brush away
the length of darkness
I let encase me.

Full-bodied,
our fore-noon dancing
in the crawl spaces
where light does not allow.
Legs 'twined messily,
a heat exhaustion
to draw from the throat
the most exquisite
sonnet of dawn;
the chorus,
two lovers in unsteady breath.

In our unity,
we had grown stronger spines
to weather any storm
that dare impede
the tenderness of our moments.

Let despair dare impede
the content of our winter.

The fear grows strongest
where it is comfortable dining.

It was in those fleeting moments;
the flash of your lips
curved upward, to greet me,
the distance between us,
pleading even as silence
rolled in, to be closed.
It was in the breaths you took
before you spoke a word,
the breath you didn't take
as I anticipated you
that I knew,
any lifetime with another —
even in this room, so small
I would rather hold drink
to drink you in —
would be a mistake
collateral enough
to splinter my spines,
so that no lover
could touch our battleground,
because our hearts caught flames
on the dance-floor
that stares could not extinguish,
all in the hours
that followed
my tapping thoughts:
thinking
and thinking,
and thinking of you.

First meeting point,
these eyes the atlas
you imprinted
in the flick of a smile.
I remember it still,
embellishments
from a gown
sailing the floor
like a riptide,
your hair blowing
in our ocean winds.
Lust, the undercurrent
cleansing next breaths,
anxiety, the carpet,
dancing all too arrhythmic,
yet with you I had danced
as the sky would
to cradle her sun.

My old habits
could be the story
that stains a glass of whiskey.

You pulled me out of myself
and into *home*.

Every night,
she ran from her demons
soles worn from the collaterals
of consequence.
Unrest, her rhythm,
bringing void to stillness.

Every night I'd wait,
by the opening of the door
waiting for those bare feet
to turn inwardly,
her plea of running no more.

May I always
find home,
cradled,
into the nook
of your neck.

My eyes
wading closed,
a solace gifted
as I watch you
unpack your bag
and fill my soul.

The birds fled
behind winter skies,
a new hue unveiled
no longer to be acquainted
of soft lullabies.

The morning dew
against crisp pavement,
this cool toned season
encroaching.

Bereft of birdsong
just the clatter of wings
departing,
who now will sing to me
in this dawning of winter?

I, the lost moon,
rising only to uncover
secrets of the sleeping.

You spilt
your lies
like a poet
spills ink.

Self Love
Save ten minutes
for a little
coffee
cheer
and company,
ten minutes
to tranquillise
the chaos.

It is a delicate situation
assuming the behaviours of folk,
each time we believe
we know its entirety,
we take a piece
out of the whole truth.

Your words are my undoing
so unclothe me with only your finest.

In search of you
my lips were cracked, parched,
through the trails of chapping air
and blistering insanity,
my lips would taste yours
before they would, water.

Lost Loves
I wish for you fulfilment
and not a moment of complacency.

Losing you,
my body split
into fragments,
only now am I accepting
they need love
more
than your doorframe
silence.

In my head
I'm making melodies
with your skin.

Even in the deepest of silences
you are not alone.

An Ode To Past
'Thou climb thee pleasure state,
rouse within me depth of feeling,
coupled to find a blushing pilgrim
beneath these layers of lace.'

93

I fell back
to the same
pillows
that cradled me
the year before
last.

She was
jam on toast
sweet,

but you liked her
for her
easy spread.

Must I draw
similar fate
to those
who hollow
themselves
in everything?

Her legs wrapped around me
as hours wrap around Monday's,
haphazardly.

I plead not for her grace,
of these drawn out motions,
her hair unkempt,

telling tales
of night's mutual longing.

A roadmap
of where my hands have been
many hours exclusive to waking up.
Oh how they long to stay upon,
this cosmetic-derelict enchantress
laying virgin in my sheets.

97

What parts
of your conscious
mind
have capacity
to resist me?

The way
my body curves
in places
your hands
perfectly adorn.

The way
my tones
and shrieks
serve only
for you.

These threads
of us
lay a lifeline,
may we tangle
our knots
creating
constellations.

Her hand
squoze my knee
in a way that
embellished her woes
of letting me go,
even if temporary,
a parting
for night only.

Typeface
Like a font
your nimble fingers
chose
most cunning scripture
versed in choppy endings.

Your smile
gracing pert lips
does adorn me
like cool embers of saturn.

How could I express
seven syllables or less
you, the very depths.

I, who desires
fated to a lasting death,
loving you scorches.

Enveloped by false truths,
shall we expose them, oh love
our congealed lies?

Unburden my soul,
oh, relentless temptation,
I resign control.

Something in me travels
innate and infinite,
many arms have climbed expanses
in aims to claim it.

Clambering under moonlight,
sheds the last light,
from days ending eclipse.

Grappling solar beams
as they dance coyly
in my hair,
do I realise;
stardust, speckled
amidst the sky,
I feel
so incredibly small
in comparison to.

May I often
lay against this brush,
and bushels of green,
never failing to embrace
how fleeting
these moments are,
and how wonderful
it is
to be half human
half cosmos.

Perhaps
if my breasts were
coupled by hands
that could hold
insecurities first
before my skin's
delicate edges,

you could appreciate
the way
it rhymes, I love you
before it yearns
for your naked touch,
rough enough
to make me plead
absolute stillness.

Love,
I am shredded
every moment
I let you
grapple my need

twine
over my breasts
'til you
screw your passion
into me

your hands
make me feel
full,
my body
tender
to the raw
intensity
your lust
promised.

Destined
to be bruised
in the aftermath
that our longing
weighs more
than our hearts.

Upon love's mourning
I held not the bandwidth
to allow your eyes to reach me
in a way that would shake my bones
if I were to let it,

only now do I see
you were the hurricane I needed
to flood the remnants of tears
left behind
in the war torn terrain
before you,

no longer do I mourn lost love
because I have found
one much greater,
at home with myself.

I deserve more
than to be the consequence
of an idle person's last clap
whilst they wonder
what function
I have possibly served
to attain such low effort
of praise.

Pollute me
with your thick
plume of smoke,
exhale it into my lungs
so we share the same dying breath.

Take me to your grey highs,
cloud me in your ash,
burn your desires
into my chest.

Elevate my body,
to the whites
of those pale moon eyes,
lift me off the plains
of earth
without ever
the movement of feet.

Your tongue flicks the edges
of your cigarette paper,
glistening
under the smooth breach.

I anticipate the next lap,
as you seal it
with the notes
of your breath.

My thighs twitch,
their movements
you so happen to notice,
your hands
drilling smoke signals
into my hair.

Addiction
hangs in the air
for the girl
whose dangerous wanting
splits skin,

— even satin hands
travel in lightyears.

You are the apple-cheeked autumn,
a bruising beauty,
crisp-bodied as a maple leaf
cradling the floor
in the gust of winds,
both gentling and stirring.

Your sweet skin glaze
swells weakness to my knees,
I plead to meet my hands at your edges,
quelled and contented.

Whispers trapped
the air stills,
trees without the means to shake,
the ground too frail to quake
what more could it withstand?
To look upon the depths
humanity has manned.

Perceptions aren't finely untangled
when they're knotted in Earth's palm,
the catalyst of further friction,
whimpers from bird call,
for it bore witness to the falling
and the rising
of bloodied nations.

How from soil could nourishment grow
in a world that demands
letting such innate nurturing, go?

For the love that crept in
like a draft in the eve of winter.

That Girl Like Autumn
Your crisp body,
bright as though
you carried still,
Summer's zest,
carving lightly
traces of belonging
onto the window.

I look at you now
and I wonder,
if your orange fibres
are to be found still
within my autumnal eyes.

Your hope grew to be
as cracked as the pillars of Rome,
tell me do you feel the architecture
of history within your bones?
The constellations pave burning cities
in your eyes,
perhaps that's why you cry
every time a star dies.

The same nebulas
that created you,
their fibres stuck within,
tell me do you feel the surface
of their charred skins?

Can you trace the lines of beauty,
though the platinum lines protrude?

Do you feel as strong
as the neighbouring galaxy — brewed,
to thaw out your core?

Excavating the ruins,
to be housed by a museum of moments.

Your iris,
the only celestial body
to be captured quite so frozen.

I am afraid of even if,
in all my entirety,
I am simply not enough.

The way we made love
planted roses
where I lay,
so tell me why
the thorns at my back,
leaves at my neck,
cause me to remember
the eve of bodies
in so much pain?

My Body Served
The banquet awaits,
fingers in place of cutlery
silent tongues,
chatter of teeth
emblematic of enjoyment,
I can almost hear
the roars of their tiger stomachs,
eyes have never been so focused,
plates never been so full
and so empty.

I spent nights wishing
for what was
right in front of me

the moment
my gut wrenched
at the thought
of her animal-like nature
luring you in,
claws extended
at the eve of your back,

I knew my heart had fallen
and kept me in the silence.

A sound mind makes for a soft pillow,
the truth a pungent pill,
lies, an acid absorbed by kin
compliments priming baseline for ego.

We are manufactured
by the home we grew up in.

I am built
of raging complexities,
two polar opposites
existing
in the same moments
I shouldn't subsist,
but the survivor
in me
always wins.

This evening
I tasted you in my mouth,
as though you were present
to be savoured
almost feeling the pull
of your tongue in waves,
sailing the shores
of my breath
as it drifted out of my cheeks
into the air.

I felt sadness the best remnants
of our whirlwind
were in walking away.

You were as persevering
as a spoon placed in the centre
of a scorching mug,
the steam dancing off the silver
alive only in flashes,
a white fire dressing the stains
of previous use,
they touch you expecting
an iced Alaska
but are singed
in your fury
to be recognised wild.

Oh to be a thread of her plaid shirt,
to nestle beneath it and feel her heart
pulsing in the moments
excitement blushes her lips,
to be a strand of her hair
when her fingers elongate, outward
to brush through the places
she is discontented with.
Oh, to be the hairspray
that moulds
her content to place.

I'm barefoot in the shadows
between bushes and greens,
with long, contorting thorns
biting at my seams.
Underneath night's chill,
a stationed moon
and its prowling stars,
if by dawn I am bloodied
can you meet me back
on Mars?

Love lust wanderer
the earth so adorns you,
attune to nature's call
windswept hair an infinity
from this affinity to roam.

Winter's fanning winds
dress your hair
as passion does,
in the cascades
of a beckoning night
where moans meet
in the mouth of silence.
Your full moon lips
open as you are,
splayed inelegantly,
but ever stunning.
Your motions ungovernable,
reaching to frame me
like a memory
begging to be kept.

Brack-endale
Sticky sweet
housing the breath
of warm coffee cups,
chairs
all too worn
from bodies idle
before mine.

Sanctuary for the hopeless,
the hapless,
yet they speak not
of the genius they've birthed
within the walls,
bilingual tongues
speaking in code,
the blazing aftermath
of rapid-cycling Bipolar,
upon the fringes
of bustling mania.

Suddenly, the coffee
becomes an ocean
to those sailing freely,
the complexion of its shores,
bronzed.

I could almost taste the salt,
kissing my feet in rhythms
only I harbour the soul for.

Novo amor, cradling
the empty spaces beside me,
'til you sat
spitting your inconvenience,
my fingers unravelling at quicker descent
through your discontent,
it was maddening.

Reeling from the pages
broken families, cyclical abuse
and you, who begged silence
holding complaint
like a sword.

Sliced words maintaining echoes,
a reverberator to observant ears.

You plead for my happiness
but are first to destroy it.

In the morning you will rise
and the world will quite simply,
begin again.

Marking almost a year,
sanity that devolved
as I was busy
diving the expanses
of you,

the you that longed for
anybody but I,
digging me out like
an old Monopoly board
as your wanderings
were totalled
of nullified means.

Marking almost a year,
I cover battle-worn skin,
uncovering the grave
I was too crestfallen to leave.

Finding summoned reprieve
in ocean's of longing
that reciprocate freely,
pooling affection
for as little as breathing.

We birth roses
with the knowledge
they bloom with their thorns,
we appreciate its beauty
from within the grip
of its spines,

when can we do the same
for ourselves?

The grin on your buttery lips
was the last thing to leave.

Doth your mind
be laden of grief,
multicoloured verses
of our last conversation?

Doth it remember
how we loved,
filling bed spaces,
limbs loosely shaped
as though there were no fear
of drowning in skin?

They who lived worlds apart,
yet living for each other.

I live on a wire
loving unrestrained,
free to fall
waves breaking
underneath,
hard to calculate
the rhythm,
how hard this time
to dive your depths,
when the truth is
I've only a life left.

Leave the confines
of doubt
that shelve you
absent of action,
lay with me in the grass,
limitless dreams await
those who dare to be
novaturient.

'I miss you'
There were moments before this
I'd spend nights broken under stars
wishing that he knew the extent
of the sting in my heart,
like a viper to a bee
he stood not a chance
once the healing had set in
giving memories not a glance.

Just as I am caught
breathless of winds
thieving my oxygen
(a thrashing
of hurricane proportions),

I too am breathless
by the admittance
most nights are idle
without a presence
like mine.

139

Your snare
like that
of an eating disorder,
grappling
what is left
now that my body
is out of reach.

I apologise
that I took your hand,
brought it to the flames
when such skin
bore not the resemblance
of scars
from any suitor before me.

I apologise
that I took your lips
crushing them with mine
in efforts to render speaking void,
enabling passion to circumnavigate
central instinct.

I apologise that your
heart caught in your
throat when you
realised
this was never what you wanted.

I apologise
for not escalating legs' speed
in the solace of letting go.

Your thirst does not abate
now that you don't drink me up,
you drink me away.

The moon,
a spotlight,
my means
of searching
for you
in day's passing.

Meet the on the border of Tuscany
drinking Carmignano
in place of French Bordeaux.
Meet me on the outskirts of Verona
Where the birds' chorus
be angelic and brazen,
seduce me with quotes
from the Bard of Avon,
my ears pricked
to the sound
of parched lips
lubricating
at each pause.

Meet me far, few or in-between,
I am perplexed by the notion
being free casts,
transfixed by the echoes
of lovers forbidden.

A bustling bar
yet you drink alone,
tell me —
do you smell my perfume, still,
does it linger every sip?
Red lips stamped
upon your decision
to cut me several shades
my preferred lipstick.

Do you see my reflection
in every fixture —
those hourglass pillars
you lean into
somber and non sober.
Indulging in a company
so much different than my own.

Tell me what it's like to indulge
when there's nothing?

The Poet
A soul who neglects
to remember
your preference
of colour,
yet remembers
how starlight
cocoons your hair
in the A.M.
before dawn.

You consumed me
like the earth swallows rain
unto its parched throat,
yet dropped me
as though it were assured
gravity wouldn't
deposit me to the soil.

You knew before I
that our last exchange
was indeed
the very bitter ending
we promised to negate,
glass tarnished our woods
departing afoot, I bled
in the crosshairs of us.

Take a bow
your performance
wielding fabrication
like a knight to a sword
is impeccable.

Tell me
did you raise your lips
to lie so naturally,
an imposé
of your second nature?

Are you simply
unable to reform
when fronted by a stage?

Your love,
catalyst
to the beginning
of nightmares.

Sweat, I shed
laying exhausted in tubs,
water encircling legs
once shaken
by your stirring hips,
every monster
endured since
your absence,
unparalleled.

I overdosed on your breath
your tongue, the catalyst
of my suffocation.

Her being was that of water
comprised of waves
ebbing ashore,
streamlined
yet refined by edge,
HD sharp
yet smooth to the touch,
an iced embankment
to hot breath,
those swimming the depths
to surely drown.

Love
A careful trek under wet slopes,
peering atop the isotopes
it shackles not.

It swims with the velocity
of loving,
the knowledge that tribulations
lay like excursions,
by the bounds.

Packing heavy for a fall
that needs only to be light.

Deletion
Removing dead cells
from compromised flesh,
you cease to exist
but you're all over me.

Taste your objective,
does it speak
to a volume so obvious,
vibrating under mouth's
ebb and flow?

Diary of a Testimony
The truth falters not upon stress,
nor the journey of journaled entries,
a silenced mouth wields the largest pen,
spills the most ink.

Midnight bleeds its brooding black,
I know you taste the depravity
you buried in me,
in the mouth of your innocent.

Don't you know
when you fortified me
to the soil,
I wasn't buried,
but planted?

I've never tasted coffee
more bold than your lips,
café stranger,
I'd twist under chipped wood
to get a more
mere glimpse of you.

Two Days
The clouds bled tears of
transparency,
sometimes I ponder
if we mourn so similarly.

My hairbrush shouts in pleas,
please brush your hair.

I inhaled your scent
as though it were housing
the oxygen
I needed to survive.

I flourished underneath your
glands.

Your hands
wrapped around me
in bear-like fashion,
as though you sprouted paws
to grasp me tighter.

I want to spend every night
this lost in you —
that I am absorbed
into your skin, in the eve
of our multiple mornings.

Internally, I begged
for a thunderstorm to strike
isn't it peculiar,
that a certain kind of destruction
could bring a certain kind of
clarity?

Your bonfire heart
loves to ashes,
a plume of smoke
warming the soul
in charcoal friction.

Yet another plague
to dismantle
those roots of hope
you're planting.

If I may help
guide your hands
to my core,
you can bury
two shreds of hope,
I'll make it four.

If you didn't feel it,
why, in my skin
would you carve it?

If it wasn't
the most honest thing
to grace your lips,
why would you kiss me
as though you couldn't breathe?

Stilled by a fire,
a flame so hot
it should have scorched
the very Earth I lay upon,
but no blaze
wrought more destruction
than that you called of love.

Eyes, withstanding of storms,
a museum of moments
to embellish icy blues,
racing to and fro,
even in elegance
she'd lost her shoes.

Barefoot along principle,
principal to her moral mind.

Of poor disposition
yet rich to extremes,
polished by all
who failed in friction
to pull 'part her seams.

Tresses torn
by the blade
of your claw
under the fibres
I was reborn.

I knew the first time
our eyes locked,
we were
of fleeting acquaintance,
our solar systems
world's apart.

'I will leave you gaping and gasping.'

Just as you foretold,
a touch loose enough
to command my body, not.

Clumsy fumbling
I hear your inner rattle,
bones quaking at the thought
you are all conversation,
no skilled mouth.

You long to feed,
feed upon your curiosity
of knowing the secrets my hands bring,
to unclothed and scarred skin
my touch chars not,
they shatter glass ceilings
not creep under covers
to soothe an ache that isn't there.

You stole her light
so you could claim it for your own,
she fought sleep in her bedsheets
because that's where your darkness lay.

I get these blind spots of dizziness
and through them I see her
versions of her through their white
and blue spatter.
I could almost weave my hopes
on the indelible fabrics,
almost touch the threads
as they unravel out the mind.

Vestibular labyrinth soon webs
a corner for control,
fragments of you painted over.

A clear canvas of reality,
the most decrepit,
it is true
you only exist in the expanses
of my subconscious.

You undressed her
long before
you grew warm
to the colours
her eyes possessed.

You,
the calm
to my calamity.

You holstered my lungs
to fasten under
the notch of your belt,
you spoke
of a breathless being
as one most beautiful.

The ebb and flow of your lips,
your tongue the undercurrent
in tides of yearning,
skin, the soft sand
lapping my edges.

And so unraveled our artful
conversation
as lips fell silent.

I long for versions of us
that long have passed.

Ultimately, fleeting ships
in night's relent,
so suddenly departing
to the very shores
that ensured our
turquoise waved drowning.

There's both a madness
and a mystery
to that which we possess,
yet leave unspoken.

Since when did our conversation
exist purely of lingering ellipsis?

The tide of my breath seeking
your haven sands,
I bore witness to the shores of us
breaking underneath the rocks
of those around us,
an obstacle course
that collided our surfaces
to break further open
our distance.

If only our tongues could undulate
through mind's filter,
leaving other bellows to the wind.

You and I
the tell of time
proved did not fit,
like a shrunken shirt
unable to be stretched to size.

The moon echoed our chorus;
la tragédie des amoureux,
forming osteoblasts in constellations,
the nebulas couldn't look more beautiful
were they not created from our collapse.

The willows nestled beneath your neck
sun beaming on your cheeks,
a beauty free from fabrication.
Trees shading your eyes
they close in solace,
entrails of sunlight
reflecting off of your porcelain skin
I tap impatiently,
strumming my internal chaos through my
fingertips.

I wished to embrace you,
but you, the evening sun
I, the crisp night moon
never could,
my unapologetic beauty
with whom it could never be.

A kiss other than mine gracing your lips,
tops of endless bottles to refute your thirst
yet she touched you
as though you were a hound deprived.

Your hands wake my internal chorus,
I bend only to sing under your touch.

Unreturned love was a waltz
I grew all too tired of.

You're the story
I'll tell my grandchildren
when they're awake at 4am crying
because they believe they'll never
recover from love.

You'll never understand
the measures of how
loves proclamation
rung in every verse,
sung in every chorus,
crafted every finish
with cursive promises.

My yielded weapon
a barely beating heart
and a pen crafted
by molten silver,
the ashes consuming
if you'd only read
the secrets behind
every verse.

I'll cherish the day my outpouring of heart
is understood by who it is intended for,

but for now,
enjoy my alien mind.

A million times, each different
versions of you walking,
gliding, running,
through my door.

Your lips of promise
hymns of regret
to greet me.

My pieces falling like torrential
downpour,
yet you held the glue
in spite of the possibility
you'd bleed too.

I lay in a bed of pine needles
the blanket stitched by
my accumulated pieces.
Hair upon the spaces
my tears have reached.
hands worn from paper cuts
where details of heart have failed,
yet you look upon me
with a gaze so endearing
as if my crazed collapse
makes me still,
the most touchable soul.

Embrace barefooted, the winding
footpaths, to grey mountains,
let the vines fondle your hair
as the sunshine ravishes it
in its golden coat.

Open your palms, catch a butterfly
feel the twitching of its wings
against your skin,
within its return to flight
let your eyes drift its movements,
so steady.

Fall in love fast, do it impulsively,
a whim that causes your pulse
to shriek through your veins.
Your heart palpitating so vigorously
you reverberate its rhythm
in unsteady song.

But whatever you do
lull it to sleep within the cages
of your mind
for what people are so aware of,
they ruin.

Your soul,
torn by conflict long-lived,
seeking only past ideations of love.

Your soul,
wrought by titanium
yet bathed with neglect,
brushed with the fibres of indecision.

Your soul,
covered by endless sorrow,
so be it for the hummingbird
to sing of your song.

Your soul,
pained so irreversibly,
yet with years at our side
white sands, and blue tide at our feet,
I have oceans to try
to aid you, completely.

When all is tranquil
and you are nowhere near
these hands long to be placed
at your ears,
my lips trailing
the delicious trails of
stardust
upon yours,
hair nestled at your cheek
in messy formation
as it teases you from above.

When all is tranquil
and you are nowhere near
my heart wishes to reside
anywhere but here.

Signs of an angel aren't always of the
white-feathered, halo-yielding variety,
they lay right next to us whilst we sleep,
often admiring peacefully,
they are the voices of serenity
in place of our internal calamity.

Like wilted desert flowers in search of
rainfall,
I would scour the edge of earth,
for a mere drop of you.

I

Slipped into the night,
silhouette dancing amongst lights,
unrestrained winds caressing her hair,
windswept, yet poised.

Slipped into the night
as though it were her favourite dress,
focus transfixed ahead
soles gracing crooked cobbles,
when would oppressed feet find
solace in destinations arrival?

Slipped into the night
air now whipping at her face,
enough to stop all motion,
looking above I found her clarity,
breathing it in almost.

Waves thundered against the rocks
her forward steps, deliberate
still, with grace she swayed
sighs escaping slighted lips,
attune to its melodic rhythm.

Turquoise water lapping now
over feet
as bare as her soul,
but oh so free.

II

A moment is all it took
to blink her out of vision
obscured amidst the grey mist.

Slipped into the night,
parting ways with land into current,
no explanation I could find
but that she was home at ocean's tide.

I lie in wait for you,
nights like tonight.

Her love was cosmic,
a soul bursting into flames, cosmic mess.

Her eyes misshapen galaxies,
one look
and a power surge struck right
through you,
yet she underestimated
the force of the world behind her.

Oh, love,
don't come back in search
of broken pieces,
I have not lost myself yet.

We live in a world
where some people are poison
and others, the antidote.

Just be her friend.

Within the silence
we carry the deepest ability
to hear purpose.

Time is no fixture in lives of the aimless.

Does love have an
expiration date?

We know good things
are fleeting and flavoured.

How many times will I feel
the same chill
before I am rendered inevitably
to its end?

Facial lines wrought with regret,
if only existence motioned backwards.

I begged for hands to grip my
unstable heart.

Sometimes
it's not what's in the
triumph,
it's what's in the
try.

She loved at such depths
because she was afraid of heights.

Nothing bares more sadness
than the death of an illusion.

I flirted with life last night,
the stars *winked* in response.

Tell me does the artificial high
drive you wild— as being present
ever could?

Tell me does its chalky stain
linger longest on your mouth
when you are depraved?

Do your secrets stack as tall
as wishes do?

I carry no desire to ache
for things that do not ache for me.

Find a love that bares not
an emblem of fleeing,
nor such which entertains
a certain thrill
from the asphyxiation it causes,
a departing of which,
is so absurdly, assured.

I knew in the pit of my stomach,
your lips extending
to touch the tip of my forehead,
was goodbye.

Denial bit into me
like teeth to a spoiled nectarine,
retracting upon the knowledge
it had long passed its fruition.

That kiss planted thorns in my gut,
I now cannot eat
without my threads spilling out,

why must you leave me
so empty?

Did you know when we sat
at that restaurant table
that it was to be the last,
tell me, was that the very moment
you fell out of love?

Fingerprinted
The last time I felt them
they were leafing through your hair.

I perspire, a troubled sweat
an anxiety plagues my throat
in the throes of you walking,
and walking,
and walking away,
my heart replies
in place of mouth.

Slamming of the door
against summer's brushing winds
I never knew I'd grow
to want to hear once more.

Clammy hands,
reveal all
your body in strides
tries to hide.

Careful,
our souls are weeping,
seeping through the cracks in the door
where you left, most ungraceful.

Your presence thrust upon me
in our beginnings,
did you plan to dock
for no longer than one summer,
marking my hand with a ring

— *the stain will vanish, love*
just as you did.

The intensity of your hate
will be proportional
to the intensity of your love.

219

Why must you bury your ache
in the booze and breath of strangers?

If my denial
no longer eclipsed
my sense,
I would realise sooner,
home is not a person who leaves
nor is it a fixture,
it is built within me.
I am my longest home
your journey with me,
as long as I will it.

Her hair
in disarray
like swirling milk
embellishing the sides
of a mug long worn,
by hands
folding around the edges,
drinking in the steam
it laps upon her skin,
unearthing a forsaken lure,
I cannot tell
whose thirst is more.

You're foxy.
Wild. Cunning.

Attached to the breast of life,
birthed in the mid may heat,
prowling undomesticated.

When you left
I fitted a door
so much newer in design
than the one you let slam behind you,
revolving mechanics,
calling not of friction
if you ever come back
to leave once again,
I can not jar it
waiting for you,
instead, my door
will spin
a grace,
weaving
your leaving steps.

All A Survivor Hears
It was not your fault
It was not your faul
It was not your fau
It was not your fa
It was not your f
It was not your
It was not you
It was not yo
It was not y
It was not
It was no
It was n
It was

225

Nothing existed less burdening
Than your reflection in my sight.

I

Fingers ridged
around the nooks
of an atlas,
far be it for paper
to ever compare.

A reference point of stars
in the cascading night.
None,
brought more befitting light,
than the glimmer you brought back
(in May).

Fumbling to the dirt,
head bowed,
knees cradling the ground
do I realise my vision
was prophecy, misguided.

Your freckles,
the mapping of constellations.
Moulding into sight,
clarity, an opaque cloud—
a sort of settled cosmic dust.

II

Hopeful breaths, nurse my ears
once too stilled to listen,
and I too ill-fitted to seek it out.
But it was I
who you had sought.

The you, earthed beyond
my many means of travel,
if I held not the vision of you,
my mantles would unravel—
merely, an ornament stationed
by lost faith.
Topsoil, the chilled blanket
to which I'm kept unsafe.

But I am comfortable now
in yielding to my adrift nature,
so be it for the moon to cry
that I may never gaze upon it
as though it is most beautiful.

My mundane layers
have found home
and buried soul
upon your iced infinity,
palms pressed cold
in our winter's song.

Fuel that desperation
for liquor on those lips,
turn it into a rhythm
of wanting.

I'll be the craving
you wake up bearing,
you'll be my sobering
tall glass of water.

These planes of my body,
vibrations of distress
fixed, internal dialogue,
in which I had been dressed.

Cloaked by a darkness,
a society inhabiting fright,
until you explored my depths
with your aiding pilot light.

Often I feel like a word,
that none but I can comprehend
other times I feel like an eagle,
who has forgotten how to soar
amongst the clattering
of clipped wings.
There are days I feel like
an empty breeze,
or a tale lost in time,
amidst all of the things that I feel,
I know each of them, worthwhile.

Her home was underneath the stars,
their glare her only light,
shuffling of bodies to and fro'
yet she was out of sight.
Her heart a place of buried hope
suppressed hopes and dreams,
but underneath those familiar stars
she wasn't so lonely, it seems.

I opened my window
to let the day in,
the sky was crying.
I felt a sisterhood
with nature,
but whilst her
tears watered the planes,
mine watered
a lonely bedside.

Your lips broke the dawn and I, in two.

The coffee licks my lips in a way that reminds me
of our mornings.

235

Even the flowers
you have brought me
have a half life,
I do not mind
their dying threads,
for they dance with me
in your absence.

I

You moulded me
malleably
into dough,
pressed into me
with the heaviness
of your fingers.

Crimped,
my edges well worn,
from several attempts
you'd yielded me
yours.

Devoured me
but left
my aching heart,
throbbing pulses below,
a body grown sour
of exploring
the normalities
of teen sexuality,
when prematurely
I'd learnt sex
equivocated
unrelenting pain.

II

Sugared me in a coat
of self loathing,
licking the base
of the violently debased
from your fingers.

You were caught
deep in flour,
crimson flashed your skin
the same night you fled
I swore you would never win,
a small child
you found delicious,
how I rolled
under your weight
sprung that crease
to flick
into a smile
so criminal,
I knew when next
I was bait.

The dips of her hips
are guitar formed,
a crescent moon
the twisting of her smirk,
her hands tree rugged
in contortion
yielding truth to her will.
The leaves
her winding fingers,
how they lace
unto lover to lover,
directionless and steeped,
almost ready to shed her colours
like crimson lips paling
under winter's cast.

Her skin, a velcro thresh
adorning legs
as she clambers into bed
to tell of satin dreams
and elastic skin
pausing only in sleep.

You dipped your back like the mouth of a vase.

Your paws rake at my leafy hair
bunching it in tufts on the floor,
this autumnal flurry flows.
You grip tight my roots
as our wild wind blows,
removing threads of me
as a daring breeze in fall tries,
but pales in comparison
to your wanting winter eyes.

241

I want the kind of love
that leaves secret verses
to find
in the nape
of a poetry book.

Lovely
bladed your lips
it was the sweetest tone,
the two sugars
to my morning soy tea.

Yet I'd come to find
you held a dictionary
of lovelies,
each looking
entirely different
than I.

Low musings of breath speaking idly to the wind;
reconcile your heart dear, love
you bed your lion heart in a pack rats teeth.

I

I owe my Father an apology,
for many years
he was not the result of one man, he
was the plethora of faces I feared. In
my childlike youth
afeared, his palms would knead me
like reusable dough.

Even now, I am learning
his hands do not burn me
into frightened flames,
they fan my anxieties,
have me pleading to grace
that I may again worship
the power of men around me
who are the greatest of healers,
my father
currently,
lending ail to my scourge
alone,
but it is because of him
that I live and breathe to my fullest,
he is the example
of what a man, and men,
should truly be.

II

I know full-bodied in my chest
other men serve to pale,
I feel no unrest
with the admittance
that nobody could never,
will never,
compare to such a man
as he.

> — *The Moon of my Life.*

Bric-a-Brac[k]
Emotional yard-sale,
the rain patters down
to bide my tears,
my home splayed
like furniture
against the nooks
and mantles of the garden.

Oh, to be a page
neatly folded,
a deliberate crease
placed by book markings.

I

I am lonely,
yet I am surrounded by people,
cascades of those who seek to help
yet they know not
the details of my loneliness.

Departing the bus
I had previously rode,
I felt a sense of gloom.
I could not place it,
until my feet graced ground,
cobblestone breaking
under heel.
The brisk of night
causing my skin to recoil,
just as the touch
of an old lover does.
As though in strife competition
with my mind,
it furled around me
to blanket me in a chill
I had but no choice
to wear.

Whirlpool of thoughts
without rest,
bash against my will.

II

Few stars
in the clearing of black,
their presence
indentations of white
to a blackboard.

I cross the street,
nearing now, closer
to the wave of my unease.

A pang of sadness
to rival the deepest
of hunger,
a moment poured
from my ignition,
I stood to witness
it quake upon the trees
as their will shook it away.

The only midnight dance
they ricochet back
into the universe,
they cannot dance my blues.

III

Dim lighted
peninsula,
corner of forest
marking my heels.

Hands, cold
yearning
to be entangled
by a presence
long gone.

Briefly pondering,
perhaps the hours of twilight
seemed befitted
to embrace from within
wall confinement,
and not late evening walks
with hours contending
to darkness.

Bedroom window now atop my vision,
homeward bound, but almost,
laced a foolish thought,
ravishing my cells
until I deemed it a dead notion,
bereft of any possible happening.

IV

I would not look up
and your eyes would not be there
to greet me,
windchill stroked my hair,
in symphonic sympathies.

Light would not
beat a relent out of feet,
as I ran, departing bags a-floored,
in hopes to reach you quicker.

The only presence more illuminating
under the shade of a sullen sky,
than crackling embers of fire.

Affairs of heart
are always foolish,
I muster.
Removing the hapless cloak
of misery
I let garnish me
like a coat
dressed upon a bed
of medium rare steaks
and pale fingered wine.

V

Why must I feed
the loss of you
by recycling
the fruits of us,
bruised and rotting?

I elongate and reach
the spaces around me,
a deep breath filling lungs,
greeted by a door
and nothing behind it.

I leave notions of you behind
in the pathway of leaves
that led me safely
back home.

In this dark hour,
the sky clad of black,
do I depart my thoughts
in compartments
I swear I won't open,
until the stroke of a brush,
or wave of a plait
edge me back.

I

Towel wrapped,
fractured porcelain without stain
my very own gift of self,
yet it took more from me
than it gave.

Alarms rung high,
processed was the look of fear,
does her blood run
to the velocity
of her madness?

Barefoot,
a throbbing reminder
of my remainder —
not totally numb.

Halls of stark white light,
a fixture nauseating
in contrast to my own shade
of red,
separating the mundane textures
of the walls.

II

It happened upon me,
nails biting into palms,
reflection greeting me
to a wallowing, voiceless.
Internal resounding louder
than audio.

I, a soul in a Purple world,
housed a-plenty of Azul.

I longed to be of plum coloured flesh,
the kind that speaks not of insanity.

Ignited by instability,
an insomnia to rival
both the grace of Moon and Sun.

Long reign the blue my skin yields,
for here we are all more cyan
than short of mind.

— These people understand

"Mind the tail!"
She shrieks, she bellows.
Flinching
under the presence of a foot
underneath a wired headphone.

Oh, madness
to which I am welcomed.
Am I welcomed?
Do we each share a cleft in the rocks,
a home greater
than this white-washed
confinement?

Believing, every instance
my eyes engaged,
ears pricked up
to the sound of incoherence.

Surely my behaviour
more normative
than that of delusion?

We sat there
nameless,
aimless,
blameless,

but tell me,
do you not see us
fit for stars?

Even the cosmos
are lonely, bundled.

I formed poetry
like your lips carved words,
wedding vow scripture
tuft at the corners,
words enveloping
our beginnings,
like your eyes locking me
into place
to be your only vision.

Set down
this book
of life
you are
continuous
in leafing through,
each day you travel
upon unknowns
that fall upon
similar regret.

Lay down
worn pages,
bind your spine
of new,
do not further
bloody,
wearied things
with far more
staining thought
than the red
that sheds
vein through skin.

For a stronger index
you must learn
not to rework
the contents of past,
but add more pages.

I can hear the wiring of the house,
feel those winding roads
steeped like ice honey,
I can taste the dreams of the neighbours
their pleas for something more,
trace the course of inaction
on their skin.
Breathe the density of the clouds,
as though they were my own pair of lungs,
jealous I am not as free to float as they.

Don't touch the mane if you can't tame the Lion.

Must I have to end
to simply begin again?

As though the winter had to ask
before laying its iced reprieve.

Crisp ivory blankets,
a cyclical twelve months
laying frost at my fingertips.
I have been rendered
too frozen to occupy
and too scorched to yield.

I am but an accomplice
when renewal I beg
for others,
meets swift decline
because it is I
who is pleading.

I have become acceptant
that thrust upon my hands
is a fear so innate
I have not the capacity
to steer it.

Must I always yearn
unsuccessful to prosper,
in both light
and loftiest
consequence?

I

You fill me up
unexpectedly,
your rushing to satiate
my morning thirst
of soya and two sugars,
but glimpsing that toothy grin
in our kitchen, so sweetly,
nourishes me more
than any glucose fix.

Birdsong further illuminates
your unrestrained kettle laugh,
jilting me to my core,
in ardour I wake.

Outside the dew fondles the leaves,
a newly pattered mess
to rival our bedroom sheets,
allotted to us by a passion
in full thrall.

Leafy greens askew
decorate the patio,
nature blooming
to mimic our emblem of love,
clambering once again

II

to the side of the bed,
gracing the carpet
as our attempts to reach the sheets
are moot.
Friction, marking you a rare dish,
my hands opening you
like a spring flower
shy of the sun.
You are tender in preparation,
and I am black with desire.

The eve
of your hurried departure
to work,
knowing that being oh-so late
deems worth it,
speckling warm kisses
against my face,
it seems each one
ornaments
how fired you should be,
your homebound labour
a skill-set,
that renders me writhing
in the hums of daybreak and dusk.

III

I dream of coming home
to these very landmarks,
where I knead my head
into the province of your collarbone,
your arms splayed out islands
decorated by peach freckles.

Nightly, to caress your skin
and taste how you've bloomed,
as our daily absence has absconded
and stars have taken up residence
of photography,
to capture all the sun has missed.

I would make love to you
in ways
that would make a dark sky
blush colour.

Petition to forget
about adulthood
for a few hours,
and again play childhood games
under the lampposts.

The wicker flame
two hands built,
but only I lay
burdened,
bludgeoned
by the roaring flames.

I could close my window
but there's something
about leaving it
oh-so ajar
so that its light
might reach you.

Though you deserve only
the last remnants
before its death,
captive still
to smokey stupor.

Could we surrender to a peace treaty,
like the one with Versailles?
Could we both don our wings
and fly mountain high?

269

The greenery taps my knee
as though it is spaced
by all that is missing
— your hand.

Her hair tossed by the coast
of Santorinian winds,
fine china sold
at a much too lavish price,
all for the glimmer of a sentiment,
time stamped but sentient.

The lights of the traffic
dance upon my curtains,
I lay here
sheets pressed
between the curves
of my thighs.
Thoughts tapping
impatiently waiting
to be graced,
I yearn a complacency
maybe I would enjoy slumber
if coupled by foreign passion
and familiar hands.

The best of you is finding sleep in fables.

I carried their tufts in my palms,
spoke of the verses you charred
underneath my skin.
I spoke of them as I would of truth,
brimming like tears from my eyes.

Only as you lay your wild ways
to the ground, a solemn,
did she snare you
picking bones of belief,
structures, a weakened corpse.
How hard dear love,
must I fall cyclical defeat,
for you to hold my spines
with no greater feat
than laughter lines?

Your eyes are bruising now
layers and layers of honest,
tales sewn
into your desperate tongue,
as you find loneliness nested
in a one bedroom sit
where home would've been of comfort,
had it first been truth,
and not blood
you'd spilt.

Acacia husks
hanging lowly
below the pit
of her trunk,
sprouting life
though in all her vitality
yielding yellow
like ripened honey,
should to her
be claimed
more colourful.

Peripherals stamped
upon the aesthetics
of those dwelling branches,
and not upon the harboring layers
of sweet progression
from foraging to pollen,
the bee reborn its purpose.

Far be it for a body
so brazen in beauty,
to meet worship
by everything
but its own self.

The moon poised its face tonight
in the shape of disappointment.

As Autumn draws its clearing,
my home-bound soul be nearing,
nestled under coal fires,
the city vacant of birdsong,
the only noise to fill the silence,
love in all its throng.

I choose the wintry nights
o' passion,
abound under linen throws,
my sheets stained by a lover
my rosebud thighs doth know.

My hands plead a remembrance,
how they shape and furl
around the bosom of your home.

I savour the sight
o' your lips on coffee mugs
cradled in its warmth,
for I know the hours ascend
when our love shall weave
once more,
like the fibers
of your favourite jumper dress,
adorning the skin and cradling
at each frayed end.

Burrowed under flickering embers
o' candlelight,
our love doth not pretend.

The presence of women like her
could have you flirt with death
only to name it a life-of-sorts,
no hell hath a fury
like the oven tip of her tongue
scaling the edge of her glass.
You wonder if the nape she holds
warmed under her grasp,
curves in the manner her body moulds.
Biting back desire,
like an unwanted lump
feasting on the glands of your throat.

I

Your fingers
spun uneven graces
licking at the edge
of my cornerstone,
concealed.

Undressing me
in a manner dissimilar
to anything before experienced,
love made not a bed here,
one half lust, a quarter questioning,
excitement blushing the very lips
you dared part.
'Mmm,' blading your wine drunk mouth
you etched yourself into me,
throwing my head back
in unfamiliar territories
upon the walls of a familiar room,
had me bellowing blows to the ceiling
meant only in that freeing moment
for you.

The moon that night you left
coy, in the high skies
hungry, as I was,
but ever full,

II

plucked from the blushing South
to wed me in uncertain North,
in line with the very windows
I twist my neck
in deliberate contortion
to view you from.

Still one quarter questioning,
still throwing secrets to the stars.

I, the stranger
you came to know
by use of pictures,
defying all rhyme
and reason
you clung to my eyes
and sought them
upon you,
what a power
falling in love has
when I had not yet
tasted your breath
in the sweet haze
of your compliments.

Tell me how I taste
now that I have stood
in the air between us,
as it tangled
like your fingers
moving hair
from my face,
your eyes
an atlas
that had found home
docked into mine,
twisting like pine grooves
of a body pricked
to every
and only
notion of you.

How could it be
you were so sure
that you framed your heart
to give away
a night close
to the eve of christmas,
tell me those white ivory
baubles you pine with
may rest upon me
even as winter comes to a fade.

I

These words
beautifully strung
dance the song
of the hummingbird,
beating blues
from her throat,
poised in such a way
it deems my pain
enchanting,
but I am ensnared still,
the empty words of men
their actions more diluted
than the salt water
washing over feet
in impending summer,
abrasive and cold.

Suffocating still
by the sweetened breath
of an eating disorder,
shelf life unexpired,
living almost as long as I,
so be it for me to think it
more friend than foe.

II

Bipolarity,
never has there been
a more
devastatingly timid,
outgoing,
housed within
the confinements
of a body, small,
yet,
yielding more
contradictions
than normalcy
would accommodate.

Not even the watchful sky can figure me out,
nature sighs in unison.

I

Often,
I feel as misplaced
as the full moon
during the day,
but I know
from my wholes
to my halves,
I am kind.
I love
in mountain loaves
and depths
even the greatest
cannot stride,
my biggest enemy is me,
and I am learning still
that I am not a place
for punishment,
I am home.

My thighs
and all they house
remain sanctuaries,
refuges taken by force
are still most powerful,
even if they are not whole,
even in their quarters.

II

In sleep,
pleading
with my mind
to join with my skin
and take back
my pleasures,
to find a love within
deeper than what I attach
onto the men and women
I know,
can only enjoy me
for my most pleasing parts.

— *You are home, you are full,*
  you are safe now.

Carnal,
your carnivorous tongue
removes
the honeydew harmonies
from my thighs,

a swelling stirs
rousing a crimson
of medium rare
beneath you,

an entanglement
that declares
my lioness
yielded below
your red wolf.

Feast upon the
honey moon,
a bear pawing in glutton,
full course a plated spoon,
creating shapes larger
than a screaming cosmo
ripping the night in two.
A part untouched,
the other face blaze-born.
Fury are the hungering stars
barren of half-light,
a many millennia before peaked
lanterns of promise,
to rival those futile hands
once a seldom silenced stomach,
settles.

I hear your breathing
pressed cold
against the phone,
if it had a cord
it would asphyxiate
your need
to wind me
back in and out
at your greedy leisure.

You told me
you would regret
the decision
to allow somebody
full access
to your actions.

You do not speak
you make no noise,
that to me
is how loud
regret
is sounding.

My paperweight holds secrets
of words I don't release,
inked on crinkled pages,
their edges circumscribed a leash.

Curved are their loose letters,
pen marked soul indentations.
Paperweight,
oh how I must apologise
for writing woes on every slate.

If you listen at the right time
you can hear the universe
course correcting,
listen through the earth's winding,
and ocean's calling,
and you will discover
your footing
on a path once covered
by leaves.

I picked up the sun
with my bare hands,
and gifted it to you
from behind enemy lines.

Take it and erase the darkness
I know you've been feeling,
take every stretch of light
as a pathway to healing.

How I envy the sea
for it engulfs itself daily
and does not collapse.

Hiding my scars from you
became my ultimate project,
I did not want you to see
the lines of tragedy
that bit at my skin,
their shrouded white flesh
disproportionate snowflakes.
I could not face
if even for a moment,
your feelings reconsidered
low in your gut,
as you realise
there was more chaos
than beauty.

An angelic wisp
of hoarse proportions
that render my need,
towering.

— *Your voice at my ear*

The moon
her circular pillow,
she wondered
how something
so large
could render her
as light
as a feather
to the wind.

The almost kiss,
the slow, unmistaken lean in.
The crevice of your lips,
mid contort.
The hot anticipation of your flesh,
mid ignition.
The warm exhale against the spaces
we've yet to fill.
Fires raging beneath us,
cracking the surface in its wake.
Black charring of earth
crowning at our feet.

The almost kiss,
our retraction even slower
than the first lean,
for if we touched,
even for a moment
harmonies of unsung choruses
would rapture us,
whilst we are safe from the fire
our world will ablaze,
a wildfire to end all fires, wild.

You asked why I forgave you,
my heart answered in place of mouth.

Your tongue has lashed
me into pulp,
the fruits of our love
blended,
I cannot bow
to your turbulence
beating me
into a submission
diluted.

The pits of your peach
turning bitter,
love is stuck to the plastic
fabrics of falsity,
all that lingers
is the sour residue
like glue to my pallet,
I cannot taste you
no longer
with the same enjoyment,
I have to spit out
your seeds.

Your love
is a paper lantern,
for a moment
I can almost see
the light you bring,
but it is not you
who lifts it
sky-bound,
your love
is not enough
to create
monumental
motion.
Your attempts
to bat it further
only diminish
the flame,
if only you knew
how to leave it alone.

A bear sleeps now
between us
you cannot fill it
with the shapes
I'm used to,
you cannot see it
wrapped tightly
around me,
I cannot endure the weight
or the heat
of the both of you,
how do I spring free
 a ghost—
how can I release
what is everywhere
and nowhere at all?

I carry the remnants
from our card game fury
I touch it and thoughts
cause more affliction
than the scar tissue,
do I remain beautiful
knowing I am marked
of you?

The sun blades
through the grass
to touch the wings
of a butterfly
languid
from presence
day long,
her watchful eyes
a ticking clock
surmising her retraction
to wed the moon
in her place,
tell me what love
can bare witness
to only
the depths below
and still proclaim
her unseen moon
most remarkable?

— How he doesn't see her light totals all he is.

You cut the cord
to separate us
only to look at me
like I held the scissors.

I cannot love you
and hold emptiness
with both hands.

You took your path
of leaving,
you cannot come back
a second time
pleading to grace
for me to allow you passage.

When your bed is filled
with shapes that are not mine
and you read the art
I formed for you,
I hope you know no longer
am I bed with loss,
the one who loves me truly
will not leave
and beg me to fight
in the name of ego.

My mouth spoke once
a love covered in honey,
now you are the whiskey
I have no means of drinking,
entrench another
with your fountain tongue
and idle action,
I am on a quest
for less mediocrity,
you cannot monopolize me
to your will.

Your face
no longer everywhere,
and I await the day
you are nowhere at all.

What I know of love, is all that it is not.

Missing you and hating you
is a whiskey slow-burn,
I do not know which is worse
the absence,
a relent I am forced to swallow,
or that I cannot stop
consuming and consummating
the ghosts of us,
whilst you devour others
in the name of forgetting.

You fuel your obsession of watching me,
now that I am invisible, I am everywhere
do you dream still your hands on me
my doe-eyed morning gaze
greeting you?

Lapping skin
as though it is parchment
and I am lost in a euphoria,
scribing type-writer
love letters
from those copper tresses,
to your peach blooms,
how still,
I steal your thought,
pleasures,
noons.

— *You bother me.*

People will never marvel greater
at your successes than you,
few will feign happiness,
few will try diminish your achievement
because they cannot have you rising
whilst they are cemented
by their own obstructions,
unknowing that you had to fold
and crack, to be now
where you are.

I

What I might tell you
if I was not so bound by anger—
you are not the reason I exist,
you could never hold me to peace
as the midnight moon does,
nor are you those watchful stars
I compare you to,
they have not left
and buried an ache in me
the size of a chasm,
that a bed of water
as large as cities
would struggle to fill.

You are not the all-engulfing ocean
though your absence deliberates it so,
you are but a girl
who has yet to transcend
the footsteps of immaturity
to womanhood.
I love you, but without you
I could live,
we were a moment
of bothersome ferocity,
it may have prospered
longer, a blaze

II

but a peace almost arrives,
I was the last voice
breaking into sound-byte fractions to keep us whole,
now I keep company with the stars,
how they giggle in childlike wonder
at plans far greater than us.

"If a writer falls in love with you, you can never die."

Perhaps that is the problem.
Fragments of old lovers lost, still to linger.

The first woman
to adorn me in poetry,
she who holds me
every storm
waterproofs in tow,
a mouth full of honey
and sobering honesty.

"Now I no longer tend to weeds but admire blooms."

— Shaunna

Faith, Absolute

This is the skin I wore
when my mother held me
in her arms
and gravity brought my tears
to the floor like a riptide,

this is the skin I wore
when like a coat
I wanted to take it off
and hang it up
in exchange for absolutely
anything else,

this is the skin I wore
when my faith in the Lord
showed me
I must shed many times
in order to become
a tapestry of shades
I wear without shame.

I need not trust anything
but faith and myself.

Not all that is worn is wearied.

Bric-a-Brack
I long not
for that bric-a-brack love,
the kind that shields with pompous hands,
only to cradle the ruin in defeat.
Coves of their fingers grappling ego,
as though you are the problem,
those structures would not align,
you have birthed the notion
too long,
that you are created only
for careless touch.

— An ode from the mouth of Brackendale

When did it become moot
to celebrate our differences,
when like an assortment
we leaf out
with fussied fingers
only what makes
for a comfortable digest?

Maybe in years to come
tales of us will grace your lips,
a hymn of regret
hands enveloping the only material
to ever grace your heart
more invasive than a shirt to your chest,
a novel you promised I'd write
but left too early to see.

I would sign a copy,
my hands still remembering your curves,
a flicker of a moment
before the queue taps impatiently
at the stranger holding up the line.
— Next.

Do not be diluted
by the actions of others
you were created for giving more
than a limited baseline of love.

We are what we think and speak of others,
is there kindness upon you?

I open my heart to correction,
that I am of the knowledge
I have long reserved
internalised accommodations
that do nothing to nurture.

Today, I expand my faith
knowing I do not carry
this brokenness alone.

No longer to be fortified
in place of your name,
this is how healing
will carry me again.

You inspire the poetry
I pleaded with Him
never to write.

The Lord may have a busy schedule
but fear not, he is always on time.

It was forever your duty
to bud on earth
and bloom in heaven.

Most nights I wonder
if my clasped hands,
bowed head,
silent tongue,
mind replacing
the broken spaces
of conversation,
do reach you.

Where do lost prayers go—
are they trapped
by white ridged ceilings
until a window cracks open?

Tonight,
under the gallant moon,
my window is open
for you.

Let's face the fear and smile anyway.

I

I resist change
much like a toddler
a coat overthrown
the arms,
a defiance
I've not yet outgrown.

These beginnings
tempered,
costly to mind's overflow
a platitude I have familiarised,
etched within expanse of mind.

Fear casts out my shadow
a picture dilapidated
in place of where home lay,
array against the mantles,
I grieve for come-what-may
denying myself the position
that I wasn't born for comfort,
but to create.

I navigated my fragile spines,
it took a year or two,
I now stand here before you
an energy birthed anew.

II

We become what we give thought to,
equilibrium breached where we may allow,
I've been in place of contentment,
been the bearer of a furrowed brow,
when I realised creating friction
in place of action, here-and-now
serves only for the stationless,
and I am much too full
to bow to my fears again.

I Depart To You
This book is the glue for my heartbreaks,
as it graces its last pages
I choose to no longer
be bonded by what I cannot change,
I release you.
> *Every one of you.*

I will survive, I've had harder lessons
and harder goodbyes.

The Blackbird roams the greenery,
those early hours before the eyes of folk
have bladed through the grass.

Here lies a letter
dip-tipped and carved
from almost empty quill,
but come dawn I vow
the refill will contain nothing
but feeling.

This was the book I didn't know I needed. The book I believed did not deserve to hold space on shelves filled a-plenty. Serving only as thoughts, rattling in the solar systems of my brain until I bellowed them to the moon. The heaviness that proceeds any painful experience does not merit it silence, you must remove the comfort of others and undress yourself of the wounds you've long held. Do not let them gather in the dust, it will prove a hard grit to swallow.

I hope that wherever you are in the world clutching this book, you are holding something else — the belief that every tomorrow will be better than it is right now.

Amongst the array of depravity, news of assault and misfortune, I hope you are moved to weave something beautiful in a world that is desperately holding out for it.

My experiences are tied and untied through the chapters of this book, the lengthiest chapter you will recognise is not about what I have sustained and let weary me, nor is it the faith that underpins my every thought and action, it is simply human connectivity in all its purity — love.

How fundamentally saving it is to love and be loved.

I entered a psychiatric unit as torn down as a city in the aftermath of a hurricane.

It has taken almost five years to reach this sense of peace, and I must admit there are days I still feel the wrath of the hurricane in my bones, but they do not splinter me into fractions.

I know that I am not the natural disaster, nor did it emanate from me. I am still learning not to let my wounds bleed onto those around me.

The truth is we are all a little battleground-flesh, we hold war torn collaterals, but we are also the ground we rise off our knees from. We are the dirt that has accumulated in our falling, and the bruises that do not hurt when touched anymore.

We are our processes of learning to love, but we are not the measures of how it is simply still too unheard of to love the person who often needs it most. You.

Thank you for choosing to climb inside my spines, and digest page by page the experiences that have shaped the woman I am currently, though I still have a lifetime to go.

I hope you read these last few words, softly.
Create your world. Do not be afraid to live and bleed outside of its lines.

I hope this is the book you didn't know you needed.